the PRINT HANDWRITING WORKBOOK

FOR KIDS 8-12 & TEENS

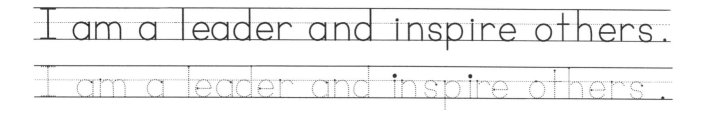

I am a leader and inspire others.
I am a leader and inspire others.

LETTERS - WORDS - FACTS
LIFE SKILLS - JOKES
POSITIVE AFFIRMATIONS

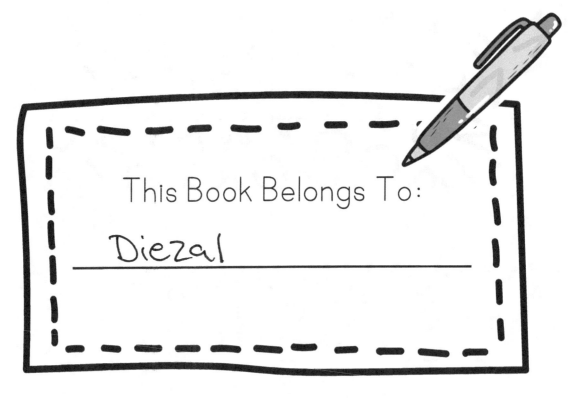

This Book Belongs To:

Diezal
_____

Thank You!

Thank you for your purchase.
We have loved creating this book
and we hope you get hours
of handwriting practice.

We value your feedback and opinion
as it assists with our next creation.
You also help other buyers - just like you,
make the right decision.

You might also like

 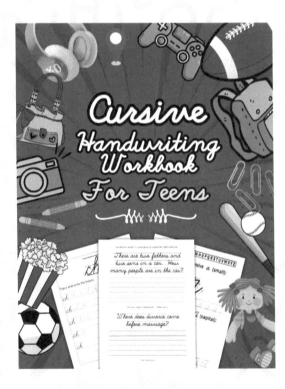

Introduction

Welcome to the **The Print Handwriting Workbook!** This enriching guide is crafted for youngsters who are keen to refine their manuscript writing skills while absorbing fascinating facts, life skills, jokes and affirmations.

In this workbook, designed with a child-friendly font size, you'll discover a range of activities:

Alphabet Basics: Start from the foundation with alphabet exercises, including tracing and dot-to-dot connections, supported by directional arrows for perfecting hand movements and manuscript writing skills.

Word Tracing: Graduate to tracing and copying a series of words, beginning with simple structures and gradually escalating to more intricate terms to ensure comprehensive practice.

Facts: Dive into succinct science facts about a plethora of topics from the natural world to technology, encouraging a seamless blend of handwriting practice with the wonder of learning.

Life Skills: This section is designed to impart practical life lessons such as time management, communication, and the importance of teamwork. Through engaging writing exercises, kids and teens will learn these essential skills in an interactive manner.

Jokes: Everyone loves a good laugh, and this part of the workbook is sure to bring a smile to kids and teens. By writing out jokes, children not only work on their penmanship but also develop a sense of humor which is a key social skill.

Positive Affirmations: Encourage kids and teens to write out positive affirmations, which is a powerful exercise in building self-esteem and confidence. This section aims to instill a positive mindset and reinforce the belief that they can achieve anything they set their minds to.

This workbook may seem demanding at the start, but rest assured, it is designed to nurture persistence and resilience—qualities that will greatly benefit your kids and teens throughout their learning experiences.

UPPERCASE LETTERS

A B C D E

F G H I J

K L M N O

P Q R S T

U V W X Y

Z

LOWERCASE LETTERS

Part I
Letters

Track the dotted letters and then
write the letters on your own.

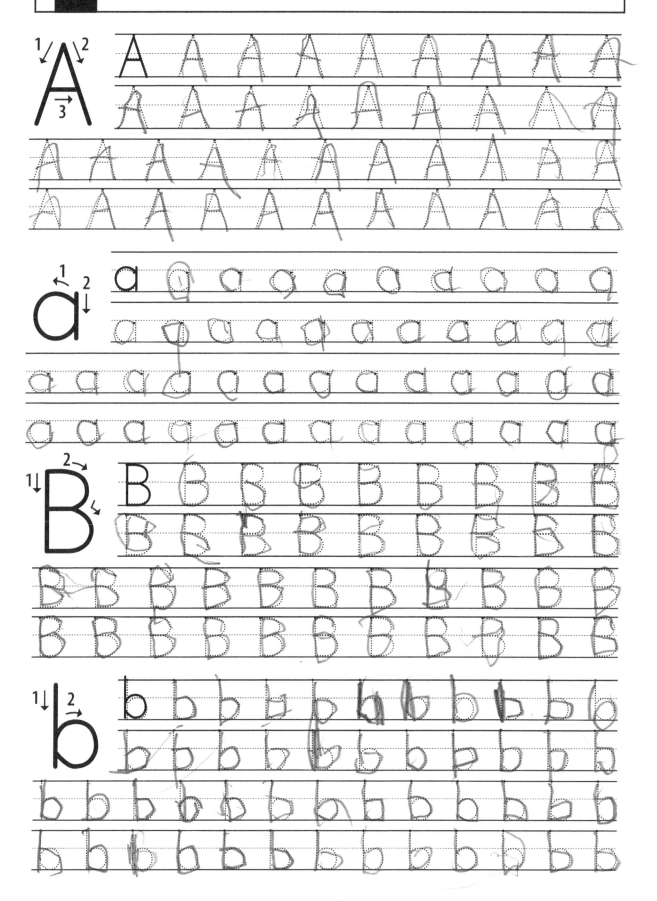

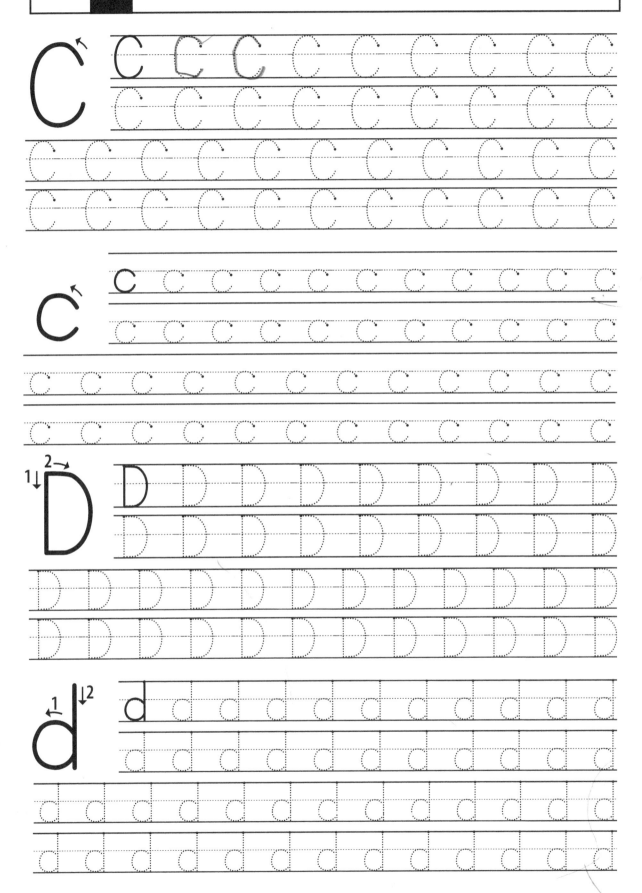

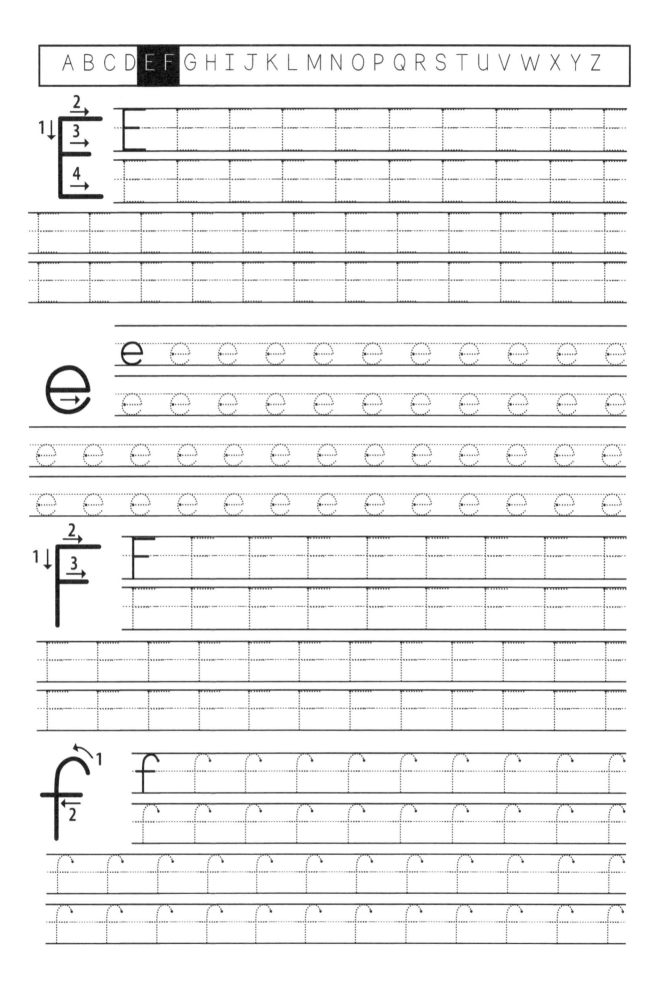

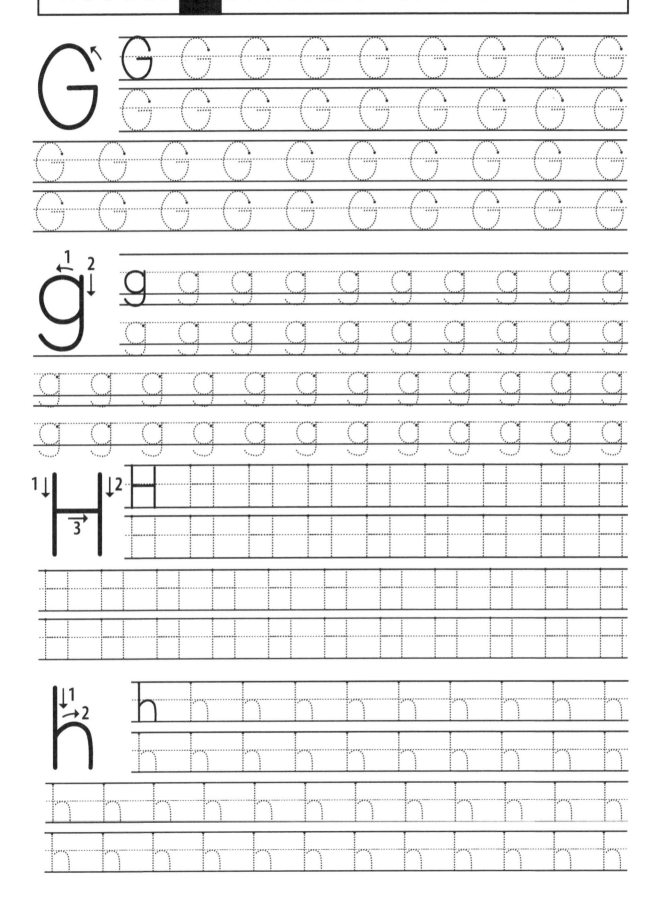

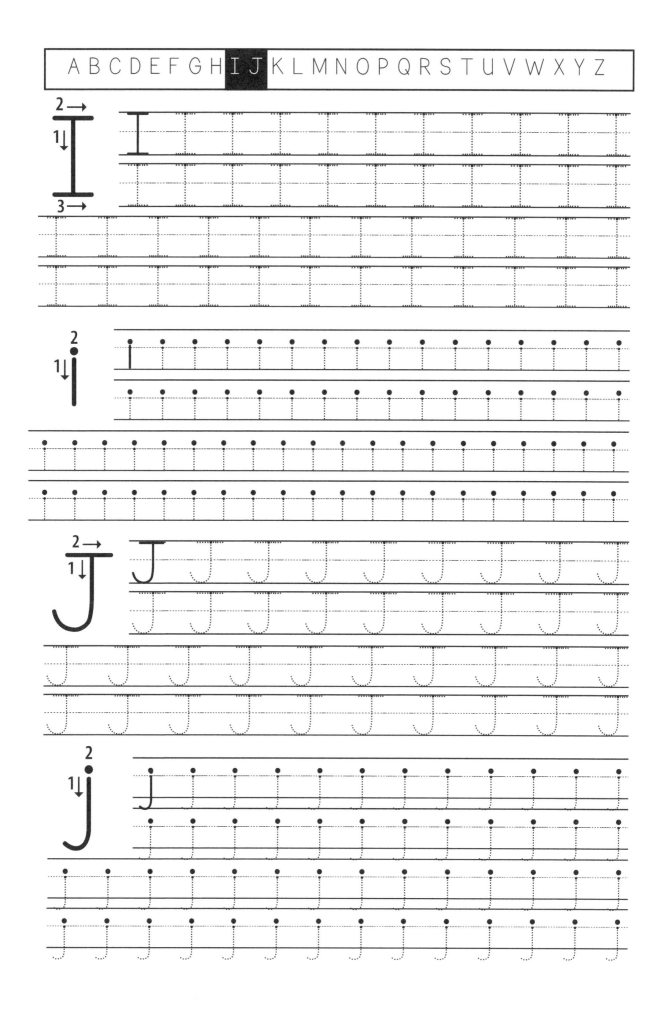

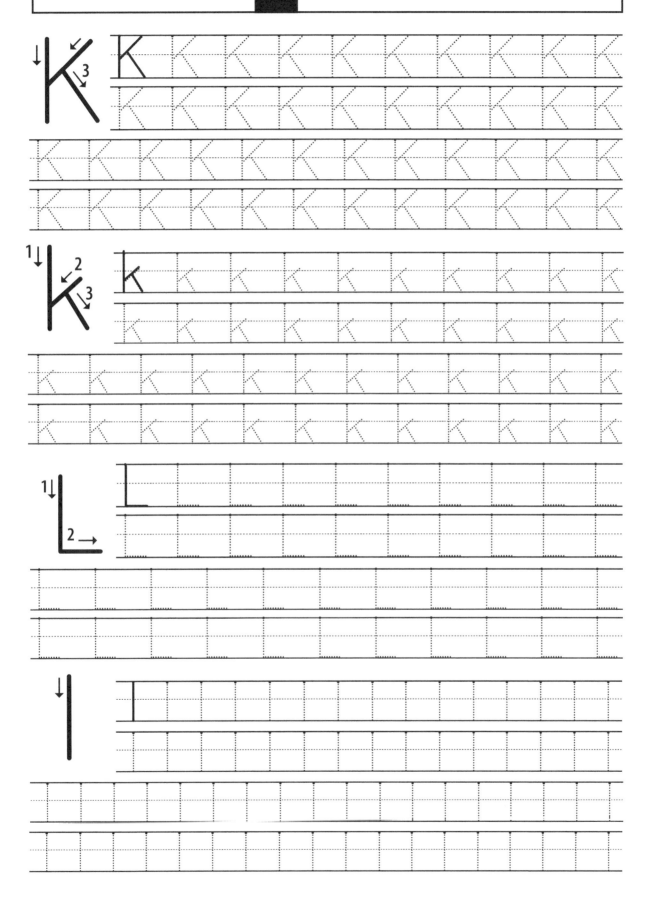

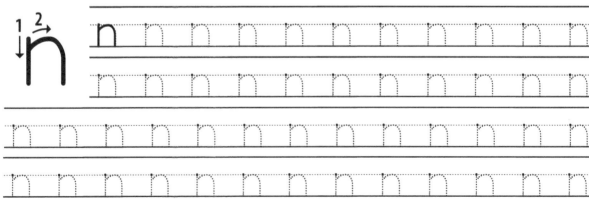

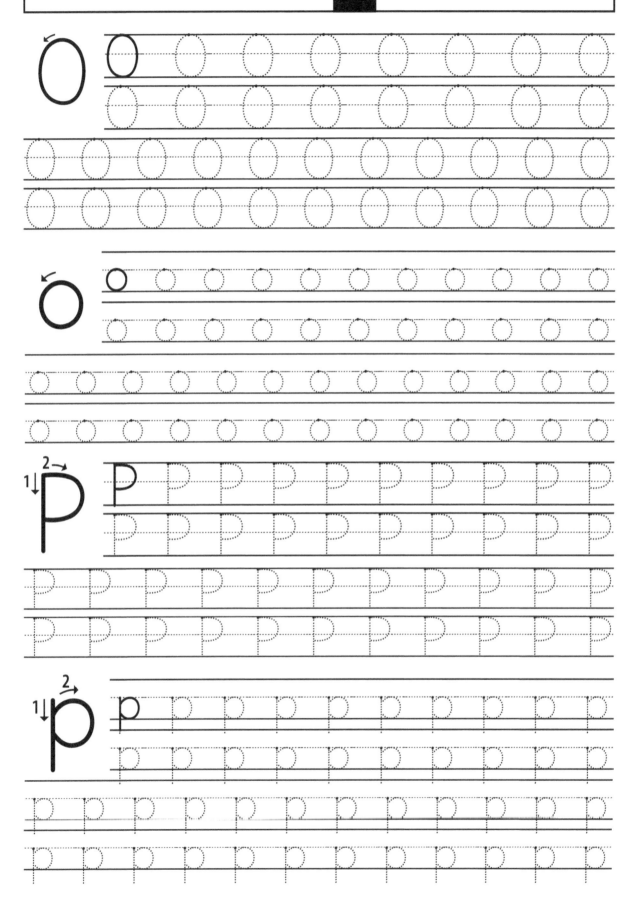

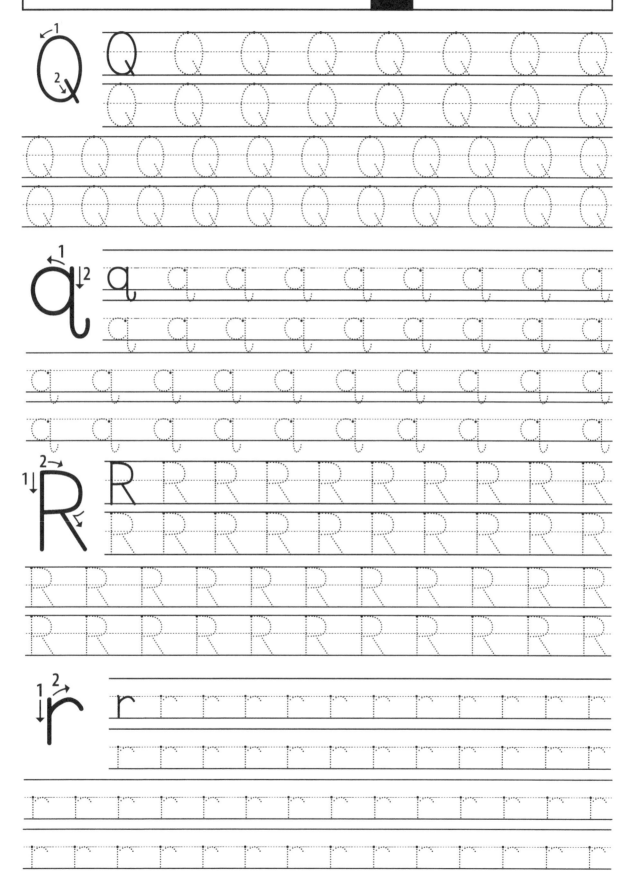

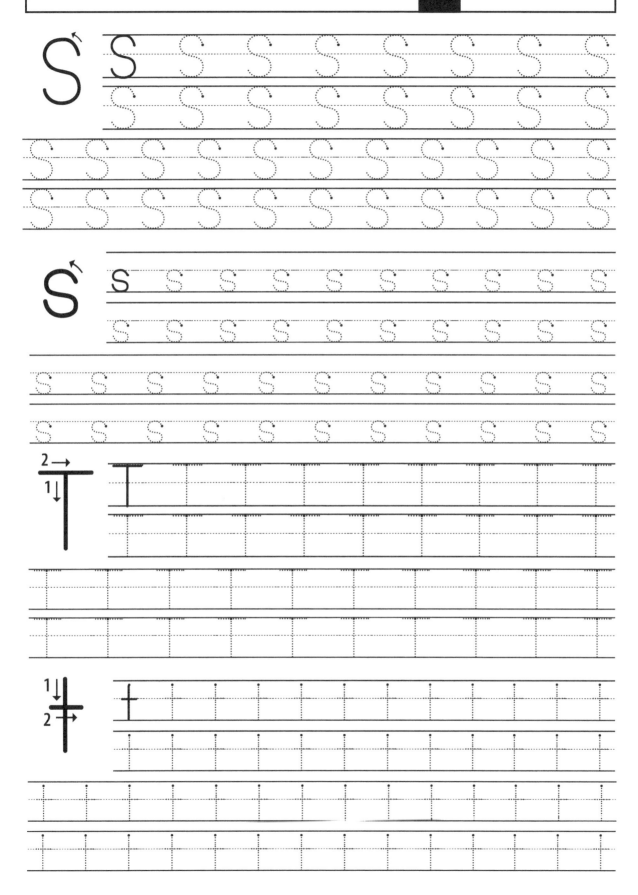

A B C D E F G H I J K L M N O P Q R S T U V W X Y Z

U U

u u

V V

v v

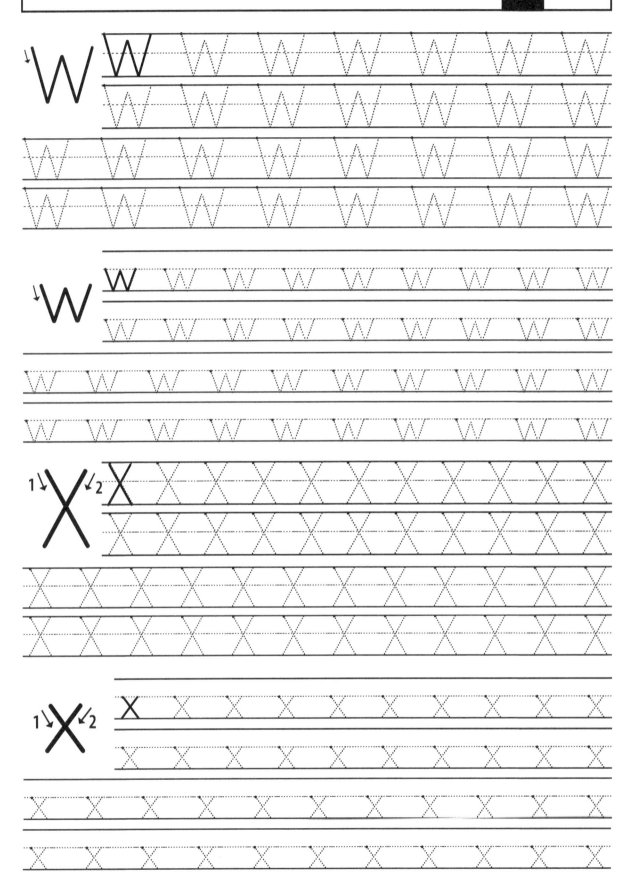

Part 2
Words

Track the dotted words and then
write the words on your own.

Apple   Apple   Apple

Ball   Ball   Ball

Cat   Cat   Cat

Dog   Dog   Dog

Egg   Egg   Egg

Fish   Fish   Fish

Goat   Goat   Goat

Hat   Hat   Hat

Ice   Ice   Ice

Jam   Jam   Jam

Kite   Kite   Kite

Lion   Lion   Lion

Moon   Moon   Moon

Nest   Nest   Nest

Owl   Owl   Owl

Pig   Pig   Pig

Queen   Queen   Queen

Rat   Rat   Rat

Sun   Sun   Sun

Tree   Tree   Tree

Umbrella   Umbrella

Van   Van   Van

Wind   Wind   Wind

Xray   Xray   Xray

Yarn   Yarn   Yarn

Zebra   Zebra   Zebra

ant   ant   ant

bear   bear   bear

cow   cow   cow

duck   duck   duck

elephant   elephant

frog   frog   frog

giraffe   giraffe   giraffe

horse   horse   horse

igloo   igloo   igloo

jelly   jelly   jelly

kangaroo   kangaroo

leaf   leaf   leaf

mouse   mouse   mouse

nose   nose   nose

orange   orange   orange

panda   panda   panda

quilt   quilt   quilt

rabbit   rabbit   rabbit

snake   snake   snake

turtle   turtle   turtle

unicorn unicorn unicorn

violin violin violin

whale whale whale

xylophone xylophone

yellow yellow yellow

zipper zipper zipper

Part 3
Facts

Track the dotted facts and then
write the facts on your own.

One space shuttle launch costs
at least $450 million.
One space shuttle launch costs
at least $450 million.

The German V2 was the first
rocket to reach space.
The German V2 was the first
rocket to reach space.

In 1947, fruit flies were launched into space.

In 1947, fruit flies were launched into space.

In 1949, Albert II, a Rhesus monkey went to space.

In 1949, Albert II, a Rhesus monkey went to space.

In 1957, the Russian space dog,
Laika, orbited the Earth.

In 1957, the Russian space dog,
Laika, orbited the Earth.

In 1959, the Russian space craft,
Luna 2, landed on the moon.

In 1959, the Russian space craft,
Luna 2, landed on the moon.

Russian astronaut, Yuri Gagarin, was
the first human in space in 1961.

Russian astronaut, Yuri Gagarin, was
the first human in space in 1961.

In 1963, the first woman, Valentina
Tereshkova, from Russia entered space.

In 1963, the first woman, Valentina
Tereshkova, from Russia entered space.

The first U.S. spacecraft landed on
the moon in 1966.

The first U.S. spacecraft landed on
the moon in 1966.

On July 20, 1969, Neil Armstrong and
Buzz Aldrin, Americans, became the first
men to walk on the moon.

On July 20, 1969, Neil Armstrong and
Buzz Aldrin, Americans, became the first
men to walk on the moon.

1981 marked the first space shuttle
that could be used again.

1981 marked the first space shuttle
that could be used again.

In 2001, the first private citizen, Dennis
Tito, toured ace.

In 2001, the first private citizen, Dennis
Tito, toured ace.

The Apollo astronauts` footprints on
the moon could last 100 million years.

The Apollo astronauts` footprints on
the moon could last 100 million years .

You would last about 15 seconds in space
without a spacesuit.

You would last about 15 seconds in space
without a spacesuit .

The sun makes up 99.8% of the solar system's mass.

The sun makes up 99.8% of the solar system's mass.

Your dog's sense of smell is 40 times greater than yours.

Your dog's sense of smell is 40 times greater than yours.

Dogs can breathe out through their
noses and mouths at the same time.
Dogs can breathe out through their
noses and mouths at the same time.

All puppies are born deaf.
All puppies are born deaf.

No two dog noses are alike.

No two dog noses are alike.

Our dogs see different colors than
we do.

Our dogs see different colors than
we do.

Dalmations are all born white.

Dalmations are all born white.

As dalmatians grow up, they develop
their unique black spots.

As dalmatians grow up, they develop
their unique black spots.

The worldwide dog population is over 700 million.

The worldwide dog population is over 700 million.

The most common dog breed is the Labrador.

The most common dog breed is the Labrador.

Dogs are as smart as toddlers.

Dogs are as smart as toddlers.

Dogs sweat through their nose and
their paws.

Dogs sweat through their nose and
their paws.

Part 4
Life Skills

Track the dotted life skills and then
write the life skills on your own.

Learn to make your bed every
morning.
Learn to make your bed every
morning.

Brush your teeth twice a day.
Brush your teeth twice a day.

Tie your own shoelaces.

Tie your own shoelaces.

Pack your school bag the night
before.

Pack your school bag the night
before.

Say "please" and "thank you."

Say "please" and "thank you."

Wash your hands before eating.

Wash your hands before eating.

Use a knife and fork properly.

Use a knife and fork properly.

Keep your room tidy.

Keep your room tidy.

Manage a small amount of
pocket money.
Manage a small amount of
pocket money .

Write a thank-you note.
Write a thank-you note.

Read for at least 20 minutes a
day.
Read for at least 20 minutes a
day .

Learn to swim.
Learn to swim .

Ride a bike safely.

Ride a bike safely.

Help with simple household chores.

Help with simple household chores.

Practice basic first aid.

Practice basic first aid.

Prepare a simple meal.

Prepare a simple meal.

Use public transport with an
adult.
Use public transport with an
adult.

Be kind to others.
Be kind to others.

Solve basic problems on your own.
Solve basic problems on your own.

Understand the value of time.
Understand the value of time.

Listen when others are
speaking.
Listen when others are
speaking.

Share with others.
Share with others.

Save a portion of your money.

Save a portion of your money.

Follow a daily routine.

Follow a daily routine.

Respect nature and animals.

Respect nature and animals.

Be aware of stranger danger.

Be aware of stranger danger.

Apologize when you`re wrong.

Apologize when you`re wrong.

Ask for help when needed.

Ask for help when needed.

Recognize your own emotions.

Recognize your own emotions.

Express gratitude daily.

Express gratitude daily.

Part 5
Jokes

Track the dotted jokes and then
write the jokes on your own.

What's orange and sounds like a parrot?
A carrot

What's orange and sounds like a parrot?
A carrot

Why did the tomato turn red?
Because it saw the salad dressing.

Why did the tomato turn red?
Because it saw the salad dressing.

What do you call a bear with no teeth?

A gummy bear.

What do you call a bear with no teeth?

A gummy bear.

How do you catch a squirrel?

Climb a tree and act like a nut.

How do you catch a squirrel?

Climb a tree and act like a nut.

Why did the computer go to the doctor?
It had a virus.

Why did the computer go to the doctor?
It had a virus.

What do you call cheese that isn`t
yours? Nacho cheese.

What do you call cheese that isn`t
yours? Nacho cheese.

Why did the golfer bring two pairs of
pants? In case he got a hole in one.
Why did the golfer bring two pairs of
pants? In case he got a hole in one.

Why don't skeletons fight each other?
They don't have the guts.
Why don't skeletons fight each other?
They don't have the guts.

What did one wall say to the other wall?

"I`ll meet you at the corner."

What did one wall say to the other wall?

"I`ll meet you at the corner."

What do you call a dinosaur that is sleeping? A dino-snore.

What do you call a dinosaur that is sleeping? A dino-snore.

Why did the bicycle fall over? Because it
was two-tired.

Why did the bicycle fall over? Because it
was two-tired.

What do you get from a pampered cow?
Spoiled milk.

What do you get from a pampered cow?
Spoiled milk.

Why don`t scientists trust atoms?
Because they make up everything.
Why don`t scientists trust atoms?
Because they make up everything.

What has ears but cannot hear?
A cornfield.
What has ears but cannot hear?
A cornfield.

What did the zero say to the eight?
"Nice belt."
What did the zero say to the eight?
"Nice belt."

Why did the scarecrow win an award?
Because he was outstanding in his field.
Why did the scarecrow win an award?
Because he was outstanding in his field.

What do you call a fake noodle?

An impasta.

What do you call a fake noodle?

An impasta.

Why did the student eat his homework?

Because the teacher said it was a piece of

cake.

Why did the student eat his homework?

Because the teacher said it was a piece

of cake.

What do you call a snowman with a six-
pack? An abdominal snowman.
What do you call a snowman with a six-
pack? An abdominal snowman.

How does a penguin build its house?
Igloos it together.
How does a penguin build its house?
Igloos it together.

Why was the math book sad?
Because it had too many problems.

Why was the math book sad?
Because it had too many problems.

What do you call an alligator in a vest?
An investigator.

What do you call an alligator in a vest?
An investigator.

What's brown and sticky?
A stick.
What's brown and sticky?
A stick.

Why did the cookie go to the doctor?
Because it felt crummy.
Why did the cookie go to the doctor?
Because it felt crummy.

What do you call a boomerang that won`t
come back? A stick.
What do you call a boomerang that won`t
come back? A stick.

How do you make a tissue dance?
Put a little boogie in it.
How do you make a tissue dance?
Put a little boogie in it.

What did one plate say to the other
plate? Dinner`s on me.
What did one plate say to the other
plate? Dinner`s on me.

Why did the bicycle stand by itself?
It was two-tired.
Why did the bicycle stand by itself?
It was two-tired.

Why did the kid bring a ladder to school?
Because he wanted to go to high school.
Why did the kid bring a ladder to school?
Because he wanted to go to high school.

What did the janitor say when he jumped
out of the closet? "Supplies."
What did the janitor say when he jumped
out of the closet? "Supplies."

Part 6
Positive Affirmations

Track the dotted positive affirmations
and then write them on your own.

I am brave enough to try new things.

I am brave enough to try new things.

I am kind and make others feel good.

I am kind and make others feel good.

I am creative and think outside the box.

I am creative and think outside the box.

I am strong and can handle challenges.

I am strong and can handle challenges.

I am smart and learn new things every day.

I am smart and learn new things every day.

I am loved and valued by those around me.

I am loved and valued by those around me.

I am respectful and treat others well.

I am respectful and treat others well.

I am a good friend who listens and cares.

I am a good friend who listens and cares.

I am helpful and contribute positively.

I am helpful and contribute positively.

I am a problem solver who finds solutions.

I am a problem solver who finds solutions.

I believe in myself and my abilities.

I believe in myself and my abilities.

I am honest and always tell the truth.

I am honest and always tell the truth.

I am a good listener and understand others.
I am a good listener and understand others.

I can do hard things with my effort.
I can do hard things with my effort.

I am important and my feelings matter.

I am important and my feelings matter.

I am unique and proud of who I am.

I am unique and proud of who I am.

I am a leader and inspire others.

I am a leader and inspire others.

I am caring and show empathy.

I am caring and show empathy.

I am a good student who tries my best.

I am a good student who tries my best.

I make great choices that help me grow.

I make great choices that help me grow.

I am grateful for what I have.

I am grateful for what I have.

I am confident in my skills and talents.

I am confident in my skills and talents.

I am enthusiastic and excited to learn.

I am enthusiastic and excited to learn.

I am a joy spreader and make people smile.

I am a joy spreader and make people smile.

I am a peace maker and help resolve conflicts.

I am a peace maker and help resolve conflicts.

I am patient and wait calmly.

I am patient and wait calmly.

I am forgiving and let go of anger.
I am forgiving and let go of anger.

I am a hard worker and always give my
best effort.
I am a hard worker and always give my
best effort.

I have a positive attitude towards life.

I am optimistic and look for the good in situations.